THE HIGHLAND CLEARANCES

Contents

The Highlands

What were the Clearances?

The Highland Region is a land of mountains and lochs. Thousands of tourists visit it every year to enjoy the beautiful scenery. Two hundred and fifty years ago there were many people living here. Yet very few people live in the Highlands today. What happened?

Loch Oich, Highland Region

You can find the answer in this book. It tells the story of how thousands of people were driven from their homes and farms by **landlords** who wanted to use the land to make more money. These events are known as the Highland Clearances. The Clearances began about two hundred years ago and went on for the next hundred years.

This family was turned out of its home a hundred years ago.

North Uist, 1895

Look at the map. The people who had to leave their homes lived all over the Highlands and Islands. Many of them left Scotland to live abroad.

This map shows you the places where the Clearances took place. Did anyone in your family live in one of them and have to leave their home?

Key

the parts of Scotland where Clearances took place

Landlord

An owner of land and the buildings on it.

The Highland clans

The Highland people spoke the Gaelic language and wore Highland dress.

They lived in clans and the people of each clan thought of themselves as a large family. They were led by a chief whose orders they always obeyed. In return it was the chief's duty to look after the clanspeople and protect them.

These drawings were made more than two hundred years ago. They show the tartan plaids worn by Highland men and women.

It was the chief who decided when the clan should go to war, for at one time the different clans often fought each other. Clansmen were trained from childhood to be strong fighters.

Highlanders were also fond of music and dancing as you can see from this painting. It shows the **tenants** of the Duke of Atholl dancing to celebrate a wedding.

A Highland Wedding at Blair Atholl, *1780 painted by David Allan*

Find:

- **the fiddler. This is Neil Gow one of the most famous Scottish fiddle players. The Duke often hired him to play.**
- **the piper. Pipe music was very popular in the Highlands.**
- **the dancers and onlookers.**

Tenants

People who pay rent in return for the right to live in a house and farm land belonging to a landlord.

The chief also owned the clan's land and divided it among the most important clansmen. Then they divided it up again. They allowed families to live on small farms in return for a payment of money or of food such as oats or sheep.

Farming families lived in 'black houses' like this one. The name was first used about a hundred and fifty years ago when richer people started to have their houses whitewashed. Black houses looked black because they had no chimney. So smoke from the peat fire inside darkened the stones and thatch with soot both inside and out.

Experts built this house using the clues from the remains of a house on the island of Lewis to help them. Inside there was a place called a byre where cattle lived in the winter, a living area for the family and a best room or 'ben'.

Highland Folk Museum, Kingussie

The poorest families could not afford to pay for any farming land. They lived in much smaller houses with little gardens and worked for the farmers in return for food.

Six to eight families lived in small villages called townships. They shared the right to farm the land and worked together on it. On the sheltered land in the glen they grew their main food – oats, barley and potatoes. On the mountainside they kept a few sheep to give them wool and a small herd of black cattle.

The black cattle were the Highlanders' most important possession. In the summer they fattened them up on the new-grown grass. Then they were driven south to the Lowlands to be sold in cattle fairs like this one.

All-Hallows Fair on the Borough Muir, painted by James Howe

Find:

- **the cattle. Who do you think is in charge of them? What other animals are to be sold at this fair?**
- **the men on horses. Perhaps they are looking for animals to buy.**
- **the soldiers in their tent. They came to fairs like this to try to recruit young men into the army.**

The Highlanders used some of the money to help to pay their rent. They also had to use it to buy food because they could never grow enough to feed the family for the whole year round. They had to buy more oats from lowland farmers. Without the money from their cattle, many families would starve.

Changes in the Highlands

Taming the clans

About two hundred and fifty years ago many Highlanders wanted Prince Charles Edward Stuart to be king instead of George II. So when Charles landed in Scotland in 1745, they rose to support him. They captured Edinburgh and marched towards London. Then they decided to turn back. In the end they were defeated by the British army at the battle of Culloden in 1746.

The Battle of Culloden, painted by David Morier

In this painting of the battle of Culloden the artist used Highlanders who had been taken prisoner as his models.

Find:

- **the Highlanders.**
- **the British army soldiers.**

What differences between the two sides can you see? Is anything the same?

Things were never the same in the Highlands after Culloden. This was the third time that Highland clans had risen in support of the Stuarts. King George's government was determined to make sure it was the last. Here is one of the forts that was built in the Highlands so that the British army could be on the spot in case of trouble.

Fort George, near Inverness

This fort was so big that it could hold two thousand soldiers. There were underground rooms for them to live in if the fort was attacked. What do you think Highlanders thought when they saw Fort George?

The government also passed new laws saying that Highlanders were no longer allowed to:

- carry weapons
- wear Highland dress
- play the bagpipes.

Another law said that chiefs could no longer hold their own courts to try their clanspeople. Why do you think the government wanted to stop these things?

New ways of life

The new laws meant that clan chiefs had less power and felt less important. They could no longer call up their own private armies. In future it would be more difficult for them to make their clanspeople obey them.

Some chiefs began to copy the ways of landowners in the Lowlands who lived in grand houses and liked to be part of fashionable society in Edinburgh or London. This is Inverary Castle which was built for the Duke of Argyll.

Inverary Castle

How can you tell that it cost a lot of money to build a home like this?

To live like this the chiefs had to make more money. The easiest thing to do was to put up the rents which the clansmen paid for their land, but that was difficult. Many families were trying to live off very small farms. They could hardly grow enough food for themselves let alone pay more rent.

Some chiefs thought of ideas which would bring them higher rents as well as help the Highlanders to make a better living. The best way for a family to grow more food was to have a bigger farm and use the most up-to-date tools and farming methods. That meant turning other families off the land altogether and finding new work for them to do.

The seaweed had to be carried ashore and spread out to dry for two or three days before it was burnt.

One idea was to move them to the coast and teach them to fish. Another plan was to employ them to collect seaweed and burn it. Seaweed ash was known as kelp. Kelp was a valuable **fertiliser**. It also contained a form of soda which was used to make glass and soap. Landlords could make a good profit when they sold it.

There was another way for landlords to make a profit. It was the best way of all, but it destroyed the Highlanders' way of life. It was sheep farming.

Fertiliser

Something which helps plants to grow by enriching the soil.

Sheep not People

The coming of the sheep

Most Highland families kept a few small, skinny sheep for their milk and wool. They were surprised when their landlords brought some new **breeds** to the glen. First came Linton or blackfaced sheep. Then came Cheviot sheep like these.

Cheviot Sheep painted by William Shiels

Cheviot sheep were so called because they were bred in the Cheviot hills on the border of England and Scotland. Blackfaced sheep came from the Tweedale area.

Breed

A different variety of a particular kind of animal.

The new sheep had been specially bred to give a lot of wool which their owners could sell for a good profit. They needed land to graze their flocks on, so they began to ask the clan chiefs if they could rent land in the Highlands. The chiefs realised they could ask the sheep farmers for high rents. This was the answer to their money problems.

By the 1790s many large flocks of blackfaced sheep could be seen in the Highlands. They were looked after by shepherds.

Two or three shepherds looked after as many as two thousand sheep. Shepherds were well paid and usually mixed some of their own sheep in with their masters'. Why do you think the masters let them do that?

When a chief rented his land to a sheepfarmer it changed the lives of his clanspeople. They could no longer fatten up their cattle in the summer on the new-grown grass in the hills above their township. Their cattle had to stay in the glen where there was less pasture. That meant they could keep fewer cattle and so made less money selling them at the market.

This is Sir John Sinclair. He was the first Highland landowner to start his own flock of Cheviot sheep in Caithness in 1791. He knew that owning his own sheep would make him more money than renting out his land to other sheep farmers. He also hoped it would help his tenants. He wanted them to learn sheep farming too.

Sir John Sinclair painted by the artist Sir Henry Raeburn

When other landlords saw that Sir John's experiment was a success they began to buy their own flocks too. Unlike blackfaced sheep, which were tougher, Cheviot sheep had to spend the winter in the shelter of the glens. Most landlords did not care about their tenants as much as Sir John. They told them they had to leave their township homes to make way for the sheep.

Highlanders were used to obeying the orders of their chief so most did as they were told. But in Easter Ross they decided to take action. A large group of clansmen met after church one summer Sunday in 1792 and started to drive the sheep from the hills. Not one sheep was stolen. They just wanted to move them off the land where they used to graze their cattle.

They drove them here, to the village of Boath. Then they heard that soldiers of the Black Watch were on their way with orders to stop them. Many of the Black Watch soldiers came from Ross themselves. What do you think they felt about their orders?

Village of Boath, Easter Ross

In the night the clansmen slipped away. Fifteen were caught and arrested. They were sent to be tried in Inverness. Only six were found guilty. Then one night someone opened the door of their prison so that they could escape. They were never caught.

People start to leave

Even before the sheep took over the hills many Highlanders realised that their farms were too small for them to make a living. Rather than starve, some of them left to start new lives in other countries. The arrival of the sheep made things worse so more families decided to **emigrate**. Many went to Canada.

Some Highlanders settled in Georgia, one of Britain's American colonies. The picture shows the governor, General James Oglethorpe, greeting them at New Inverness.

The Granger Collection, New York

Many young men decided to join the British army. Sometimes a chief formed his own Highland regiment and they joined that. This officer is from the 79th Regiment. A thousand men from Lochaber joined it in 1793 when they were turned out of their homes.

Emigrate

To go to live in another country.

Some landowners still hoped that new work could be found to stop people leaving the Highlands. In 1801 the government sent an engineer called Thomas Telford to see what could be done. He said that roads, bridges and a new canal should be built. These would make it easier to send things like fish and kelp to the south, and that would help the Highlanders make a better living. Meanwhile they could be paid to build them.

The building work went on for more than twenty years. This is the Caledonian Canal.

The Caledonian canal linked the east coast at Inverness to the west coast at Fort William. It joined up three inland lochs.

Unfortunately the canal was not used as much as Telford expected. The roads and bridges were well used, but they did not bring new factories and fishing ports to the Highlands. The people remained poor. The best way for a landlord to make money was still to turn the land over to sheep.

The Sutherland Clearances

Plans for improvement

Dunrobin Castle is in Sutherland. Elizabeth, Countess of Sutherland had inherited it when she was only six years old. She and her husband, the Earl of Stafford, were the richest couple in Britain. Most of the people in Sutherland were her tenants.

Dunrobin Castle

The Earl of Stafford

The Countess of Sutherland

The Countess did not spend time looking after the land herself but paid a **factor** to keep a list of the tenants and collect the rents for her.

The Countess's parents had died when she was a child and she had been sent to Edinburgh to be educated. Neither the Earl nor the Countess spoke Gaelic and knew nothing about the way of life in the Highlands.

Most of the year they lived in London and at parties, other Scottish landlords like Sir John Sinclair, told them about how they could improve their Highland estate, make it more profitable and sell their Scottish wool for high prices in Europe. In 1805 the Countess and her son arrived at Dunrobin Castle for a holiday. They asked the factor to show them the rent books for the farms and cottages on the estate.

Factor

The person who managed the estate when the owner was away.

The rents had not been increased for many years and the tenants lived on some of the best **grazing land**.

The Countess decided to bring the Cheviot sheep to Sutherland. She would move the tenants to new villages which would be built with the profits from the wool. She did not think about where the tenants would go, before the new villages were built.

Helmsdale was one of the villages.

Find:

- **the harbour paid for by the Countess.**

At Brora, a coal mine and brickworks were opened.

Which jobs do you think the tenants would like best – their old ones or their new ones?

Grazing land

Rich grassland, where the sheep could find all their food.

Patrick Sellar

The Countess employed two people to carry out her improvement plans, a factor called William Young and a lawyer called Patrick Sellar.

Patrick Sellar

Patrick Sellar owned a farmhouse at Syre. He wanted to start his own sheep farm, so was very keen to clear the tenants off the land as quickly as possible.

He told the factors:

- only to give them a week's notice
- not to allow them to stay to harvest their crops
- to throw their belongings out of their houses and **evict** them if they refused to go
- to burn their houses so that they could not return.

Patrick Sellar's house

Evict

Turn people out of their homes.

Eyewitness accounts

There are many **eyewitness** accounts of what happened next.

Betsy Mackay was 16 years old. Many years later she said:

The burning party came round and set fire to our house at both ends, reducing to ashes whatever remained within the walls. The people had to escape for their lives, some of them losing all their clothes except what they had on their backs. The people were driven away like dogs who deserved no better.

George Macdonald watched his father try to save parts of their house.

He tried to save a few pieces of wood out of the burning house, which he carried to the river about half a mile away, and there formed a raft with it. His intention was to float the wood down the stream and build a kind of hut somewhere to shelter his weak family, but the burning party came that way and seeing the timber, set fire to it, and soon reduced the whole to ashes.

Eyewitness

Somebody who is present at an event and can tell other people what happened.

A monument to Donald Macleod

In his book called *Gloomy Memories*, Donald Macleod described how Patrick Sellar piled firewood round William Chisholm's house, even though his wife's mother, who was nearly 100 years old, was still inside.

Donald Sage was minister at Achness who tried to comfort the poor farmers. He remembered:

Thither they were driven, at a week's warning. On the day of their removal they would not be allowed to remain, even on the bleakest moor and in open air, for a distance of twenty miles around

D.S

Even when all the people had gone, he found fires still burning.

The flames of the preceeding week still slumbered in the ruins, and sent up into the air spiral columns of smoke; whilst here a gable and there a side wall, undermined by the fire burning within them, might be seen tumbling to the ground.
The sooty rafters of the cottages, as they were being consumed, filled the air with a heavy and most offensive odour.

D.S

Patrick Sellar on trial

All over Sutherland, people decided they had to do something about Patrick Sellar and his methods.

They signed a letter to the Countess in London telling her what was happening. She passed the letter to the **sheriff**. His deputy, Robert McKid, travelled to Strathnaver, where the worst burnings had taken place, to meet the eyewitnesses.

This is the Tollbooth at Inverness. When Robert McKid returned, he arrested Patrick Sellar and put him into this prison. He put him on trial for causing the deaths of three people.

Sheriff

The person responsible for seeing that the law was kept.

At the trial there were many witnesses from the glens. However, Patrick Sellar brought his friends to speak up for him. Most of them were landowners like himself, who thought the improvements on the farms were a good thing.

They told the court:

- He was an honest man who would not hurt anyone.
- Mr McKid was dishonest and had made up some of his **evidence**.
- The three people had died because they were old, not because they had been evicted.
- The people of the glen could not be trusted.

Evidence

Information given in a court of law.

The trial took all day and half the night, but the court listened to the landowners, not the poor farmers. Patrick Sellar was found not guilty and set free.

This plaque was put up a few years ago by people alive today who think that Patrick Sellar was a guilty man.

What do you think?

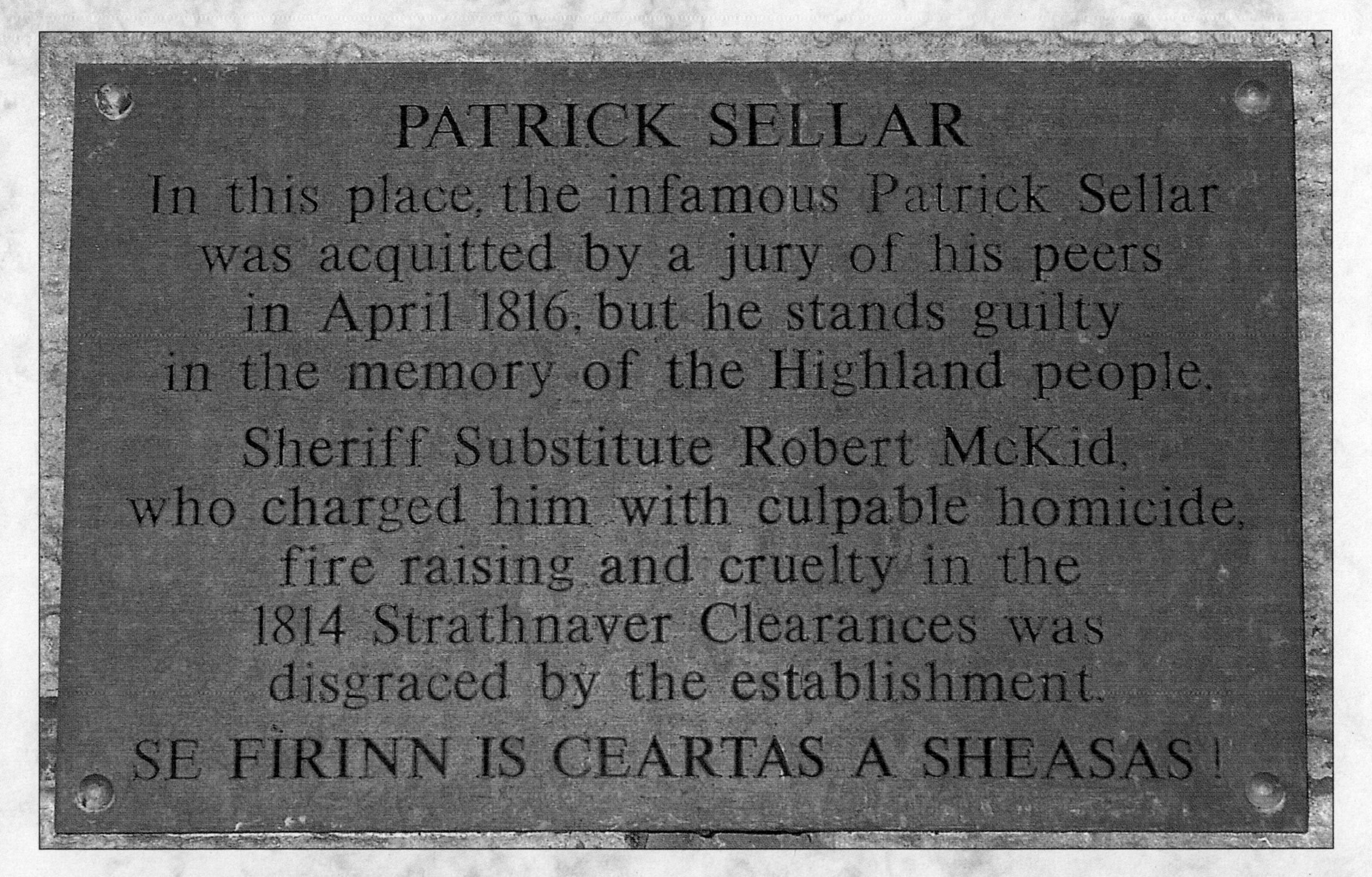

The Potato Famine

Evictions continued all over the Highlands, but there was worse to come. The farming families had been sent to live on crofts, near the coast and had to grow all their own food. Many families lived largely on potatoes.

Planting potatoes in Wester Ross

In 1846, there was a **famine**. The potato crop had a disease called blight which killed off all their plants. This meant that they had no seed potatoes to plant out the following year.

The blight made many more families decide they had to move.

There were many different ideas about what to do.

- Rich people were asked to give money to charities who would use it to buy food.
- Landowners were made to supply a regular ration of oats to their tenants.
- Women were told to sell their knitting if they wanted a ration of oats.
- Men were told to join road building gangs if they wanted a ration of oats.
- Families were offered the fare to Canada and persuaded to leave Scotland forever.

Destitution Road, Dundonnell Forest

The roads built by the starving crofters were called 'destitution roads' because they were built by people who had no other way to support themselves.

Famine

A time when many people starved to death because they had no food.

Queen Victoria

More changes in the Highlands

Rich people from London and Edinburgh began to take their holidays in those parts of the Highlands where people had moved from the land. They liked to dress up in tartan, walk in the hills, draw, fish for salmon and shoot deer. Some Highlanders found new jobs as **gillies**.

The Monarch of the Glen, Landseer

This picture of a red deer was painted by one of Queen Victoria's favourite artists and given the name of the Monarch of the Glen.

Gillies

Servants. They had to show the visitors where deer, salmon and grouse lived.